Robert Bringhurst

The Beauty of the Weapons

Selected Poems 1972–82

COPPER CANYON PRESS

First published in Canada by McClelland and Stewart,
Limited in 1982. First U.S. edition by Copper Canyon
Press published in 1985.
ISBN 0-914742-90-6

The publication of this book is made possible by a grant
from the National Endowment for the Arts.

Copper Canyon Press is in residence with Centrum
at Fort Worden State Park.

Photo of the author by Beatrice Dowd.
The type in this book is Aldus.

Copper Canyon Press
Post Office Box 271
Port Townsend, Washington 98368

In memory of friends,

F. William Reuter III, 1942 – 76,

and Krista Maeots, 1945 – 78,

who followed the mind as far into

the dark as it led them.

PREFATORY NOTE

Most of these poems have appeared previously in more or less elusive books, chapbooks, and broadsides issued by small presses in Canada and the United States over the last ten years. The approximate dates of first publication are noted here in the table of contents. Some form of chronological reference seemed desirable, and this one has at least the merit of verifiability, though I hope it does not suggest undue reverence for particular states of the text. Most of the poems are products more of oral composition than of writing, and have survived into this selection only with repeated performance as a test. Some of them have changed a good deal in the process. It seems to me they exist in the voice, to which the page, though we enshrine it, is in the right order of things a subservient medium. On this view, a man's selected poems ought to mean not his washed and dressed historical record but his living repertory: not a catalogue of the animals he has named but a festival of those who are still speaking. A book, like a performance or recording, no matter how illustrious the audience or how formal the occasion, is only one more draft.

The books and a few of the magazines in which these pieces first appeared are named in customary detail at the end of the book. To a number of patient editors, incurable publishers and critically outspoken friends I have grown yearly more indebted and more grateful. And to several tough and beautiful women.

My editor in this case, Dennis Lee—who would strike this sentence at once, if I let him—knows the extent of his contribution to the book and may measure by that not only my thanks but my astonishment and admiration. The glossary of oddities and complications to be found on page 155 was prepared at his request for this edition.

Not least, I am grateful to several people and institutions—notably the Canada Council, Miki Cannon Bringhurst, and Ron and Jean Huntington—whose money has fed me or whose houses have housed me while I monkeyed and fussed with the words.

*

The poems, as must be obvious, are the product of a life negligently scattered over too much ground. Canada, to which I first came in 1953, when I was six, has taken me in time and again as I arrived sullen and ungracious, bearing fragments of strange tongues and the remnants of strange visions. We had been at it a long time before I grudgingly admitted that the place was home. I would like belatedly to record that I am grateful to have had one. All the more for that, the words that come to mind when there are speeches being made are the Rinzai masters' admonition, that the true man has no name and no address.

Garibaldi, British Columbia
1982

CONTENTS

THESE POEMS, SHE SAID

These poems, these poems,
these poems, she said, are poems
with no love in them. These are the poems of a man
who would leave his wife and child because
they made noise in his study. These are the poems
of a man who would murder his mother to claim
the inheritance. These are the poems of a man
like Plato, she said, meaning something I did not
comprehend but which nevertheless
offended me. These are the poems of a man
who would rather sleep with himself than with women,
she said. These are the poems of a man
with eyes like a drawknife, with hands like a pickpocket's
hands, woven of water and logic
and hunger, with no strand of love in them. These
poems are as heartless as birdsong, as unmeant
as elm leaves, which if they love love only
the wide blue sky and the air and the idea
of elm leaves. Self-love is an ending, she said,
and not a beginning. Love means love
of the thing sung, not of the song or the singing.
These poems, she said. . . .
                              You are, he said,
beautiful.
          That is not love, she said rightly.

Hunters & Pilgrims

Tzu-ch'an answered: When spiritual beings have a place to return to, they need not become malicious. I have allowed them a place to return to.

Tso-ch'iu Ming, *Tso Chuan*

He wanted to say his prayer, but could remember nothing but the multiplication table.

Hans Christian Andersen, *The Snow Queen*

THE BEAUTY OF THE WEAPONS

El-Arish, 1967

A long-armed man can
carry the nine-millimeter
automatic gun slung
backward over the right shoulder.

With the truncated butt
caught in the cocked
elbow, the trigger
falls exactly to hand.

These things I remember,
and a fuel-pump gasket cut
from one of the innumerable
gas masks in the roadside dump.

I bring back manuscript picked
up around incinerated trucks
and notes tacked next
to automatic track controls.

Fruits of the excavation.
This is our archaeology.
A dig in the debris
of a civilization six weeks old.

The paper is crisp and brittle
with the dry rock and the weather.
The Arabic is brittle
with the students' first exposure

to air-war technology and speed.
Ridiculous to say so, but
the thought occurs,
that Descartes would be pleased:

the calculus is the language
of the latest Palestinian
disputations
in the field of theology.

The satisfying feel
of the fast traverse
on the anti-aircraft guns
is not in the notes.

It lies latent and cool
in the steel, like the intricate
mathematics
incarnate in the radar:

the antennae folded and rolled
like a soldier's tent,
sweeping the empty
sky and the barren horizon,

the azimuth and the elevation,
sweeping the empty air
into naked abstraction,
leading the guns.

The signal is swirled until it
flies over the lip like
white, weightless
wine from a canteen cup.

Invisibly, the mechanism sings.
It sings. It sings like a six-ton flute:
east, west, always the same
note stuck in the rivetless throat.

And yet, a song as intricate
as any composition by Varèse,
and seeming, for the moment, still
more beautiful, because,

to us, more deadly.
Therefore purer, more
private, more familiar,
more readily feared, or desired:

a dark beauty with a steel sheen,
caught in the cocked
mind's eye and brought
down with an extension of the hand.

SONG OF THE SUMMIT

The difference is nothing you can see – only
the dressed edge of the air
over those stones, and the air goes

deeper into the lung, like a long fang,
clean as magnesium. Breathing
always hollows out a basin,

leaving nothing in the blood
except an empty
cup, usable for drinking

anything the mind finds – bitter
light or bright darkness or the cold
corner of immeasurable distance.

This is what remains: the pitted blood
out looking for the vein,
tasting of the tempered tooth and the vanished flame.

ARARAT

The deepening scour of the keel across this
granular water. Nothing more. The fissure
through the estuary five
thousand feet over the headwater. These
are the real mouths of rivers: the teeth,
not the slough and the rattles.

We have been here
before, eating raw air, but have always
forgotten,

all day eating the air the light
impales,
stalking the singular animal.

I no longer remember whether a fish
or a bird. Nor whether its song or its silence
is what we were listening for. I remember
a bow in a black tree, and a snowbound
ploughshare.
Here is no spoor and no flotsam
timber. Simply the blue sliding into
the furrow on the tilting light, and the violet
sky always casting the same white shadow.

A QUADRATIC EQUATION

Voice: the breath's tooth.
Thought: the brain's bone.
Birdsong: an extension
of the beak. Speech:
the antler of the mind.

FOUR GLYPHS

I

Tlaloc's jacket was sleeveless
and made out of cloud.
A string of green stones
sank into his shoulders.
The tall blue sky was his brain.

Tlaloc planted the rain.
He planted it loud
as boulders
and quiet as butterflies' bones.
And in a time to come he will reap it.

II

The wind is the feather of the lizard that the lizard
never wears,
         and the cloak of the kidnapped king,
the rain's roadsweeper, and the wind
is the god in his ocelot anklets:
                the wind
leaps out of the mountain, wind with white teeth
and bright talons, light and dark wind within wind,
air in the air's heart and arteries, dark
wind in the vein under live tissue of wind,

bones made out of bright air and the dark air
swollen around them, tendon and flexed
muscle of wind, air like white onyx set in sockets
of the wind and the light on them, stopped light,

caught the way the sunlight slides over garnet
or cabochon sapphire:
                              wind
pounces out of the mountain, the wind
leaps out of the overturned shield.

III

The hummingbird's tongue
under the sun's black anther,
fire taking the sky's measure,
light's core soaring over
blue air, wave, rock and water,
over eagle-cactus, pine,
. and the spiked dust of the summer highlands,

bright blade of blue sunlight
over the stone,
spalled off the solid block
of the sky's light like a smoke-thin
razor of obsidian
or an unseen wing.

IV

Tezcatlipoca at Tula, the Toltec
Smoking Mirror, can be looked for in four
directions:

Red in the East, the fertile light, the flayed
bright water in the canebrake, quivering
flesh of the air alive over the limber reed.

Black in the North, the vanished absolute
fruit of the fire, the cold flint flat between
two hands, tasting of death and the dead land.

White in the West, where the wind lies
over gold water and under a beam
like flame on a flat stone, under hewed timber.

Blue to the South, under the sun's beak, where
the rabbit hears the iridescent bird.

THREE DEATHS

Itzehecaian, Tlalocan, Ilhuicac

Through the chipped air and black blades of the wind
to the nine lands. No mountain image or sunlight
or starlight or bright rain,

the blood-cage and the blood
homogenizing into
one dampness: the death by disease.

The veined green, the garden submerged in the gunmetal
twilight over Orizaba's icecap, the unmapped
air above the last black moss:

death in open water, death by the loose stone,
by lightning, by hunger, by darkness,
never by weakness, but alone.

The star's core, the taut marrow of light,
the white severing: death by turning
the back on nothing and spinning,

facing out always at them all.

THE SUN AND MOON

In the night's darkness there was once no moon,
and no sun rose into the dawn's light, no sun
sucked the color from the grass.
No moon opened the empty womb,
no moon frosted water, leaf and stone.
No sun burned into the upturned eye at noon
or polished the sparrowhawk's skull
or the coyote's bone.

Each night a girl's lover came to her,
hidden from her sight,
when the light was gone from her night fire.

Each day she searched the eyes
of the young men, certain she would recognize
the daylit shape of eyes whose blind,
dumb gleam in the midnight licked
like a tongue into the corners of her blood.

A month of days, and her lover's secret stood.

Waiting, one night, willing to wait
no longer to know her lover by day, by sight,
she blackened her hands with the soot
from her evening fire.

In the morning she looked for her lover and found
the marks of her hands on the back of her brother.

She ran. He ran after her,
over the sea's cold meadow, the grass,
the mountains, the trees, to the earth's end
and over.

She became the flaming sun,
and her brother became the husk of the moon,
to chase her, to come to her, brother and lover,
again.

Her virgin blood flows in the dusk
and she wipes it away at dawn.
Her evening fire burns in the dusk
and her morning fire in the dawn,
and he comes out looking, over sea and land,
when her evening fire grows cold and black,

and the marks of her hands
are still on his back.

THE GREENLAND STONE

Gods immersed in the masked
North American air
vanish like cryolite,
vanish like the kayak's
white stone anchor hitting
bright blue arctic water.

The snowfall in the stone
clears when the lightfall slows
the way the heart's thought, the eye's
mossy chalcedony
and the mind's wet marrow
clarify when it quickens.

POEM ABOUT CRYSTAL

Look at it, stare
into the crystal because
it will tell you, not
the future, no, but
the quality of crystal,
clarity's nature,
teach you the stricture
of uncut, utterly
uncluttered light.

STONE-LATHE AND WING

The spindrift of the stone
over the motion of the chisel,
latticed into the crosscut of the light,

and the glistening umber
dust off the caught
wing of an uncaught moth

climbing the thumb,
a pumice with a glint like
agate evaporating,

agate reassembling the air.

STUDY FOR AN ECUMENICAL WINDOW

Moses and Mohammed knew
the long hollow in the silence through
the script in the star-eaten stone
and the incessant alternation
of the new-honed
light and the rust-pocked, chipped, uneven
edges of the sun. They saw beyond
the carbon at the heart of it, diamond
and damascene steel, the crystal
riveted into the bone
that has been
cut to fit the socket of the hand.

They looked through oxide and scale,
oakbark, hide, nail, the enamel
over the live nerve. Yes, certainly, they knew
the taste of marrow,
visions that grow in the bone, things seen
in the sap before it is frozen,
in the hard unclouded fluid.
Moses and Mohammed
saw the blood before the air eats
into its essence, when the light sits
not quite on it but
about it, without weight.

Moses and Mohammed, yes,
they saw the surface
that is deeper than the water,
listened to the light
and the undertow's sound.
They knew the word will congeal around
the heart and in that instant it is

brighter than at any time later,
tighter than the crystal, finer
than the blade that has been sharpened
into effervescence,
ground down an atom at a time.

They saw inside the iridescence,
listening to the clinkstone cut
the wind, and watching the water shut
the white light out and into colors.
Underneath, they knew the blood's
similar
surface in the darkness
of the artery, the darkness
gathered in against it, not
quite on it but about it, without weight,
fluctuating, humming under
the pulse in the incessant

alternation, the insistent
oxidation under the iced-over
heaps of decayed leaves and abandoned
timber: a darkness that is
razor-like and ragged, like
the stone of the circumcision,
the die's edge, the final incursion
of the chisel, the precise place
where the sculpture grows
out of its base. Flint for the light to strike;
backdrop for the diamond's
museum-case.

A LESSON IN BOTANY

Consider it: in the mountains
of Malaya, on the mammoth grape:
the masterpiece, a twenty-four-pound
flower, its diameter
twenty-eight inches in full bloom.
A triumph! Leafless, asepalous,
rootless and stemless: pure flower.

Its adhesive seeds grow
tendrils into the Tetrastigma
vine. It takes nine months to open
fully and stays open seven days.
It has five petals, reddish
brown and often mottled. All
its organs are dead-center
in a blood-colored, lidded cup.

Consider, furthermore, its smell,
which is precisely that of
twenty-four fully opened
pounds of rotting meat; the method
of its pollination: carrion-
eating flies; and of its seed-
dissemination: fruit rats.

Sir Thomas Stamford Raffles,
the man who planted the Union
Jack on Singapore, has given it
its name: it is *Rafflesia
arnoldi*. This, of course,
is history. *Rafflesia
arnoldi* by any other
name would be *Rafflesia
arnoldi* as we know it and
the largest flower in the natural world.

THE FISH WHO LIVED TO TELL ABOUT IT

Once there was one fish only. It didn't have any
memories. Presently it died.

Then there were two fish. They fought. They got
really very good at it.

Elsewhere three fish. Three fish were
enough: they could circle in the water.
They ate each other.

Four fish. First they had a brawl, then
they had two simultaneous fights, then a one-ring
circus. One of them got out early,
leaving three. The meek do, indeed, from time to time
inherit the territory (wishing well in this case)
for a little while. Then they start to dream. They are
meek; they have seen fighting.

SOME CIPHERS

If I say
$1 + e^{\pi i} = 0$,
I have recorded a rather
elaborate but arguably beautiful way
of reducing unity to zero.

If, however, I say
$1 + 1 = 2$, or 1
$+ 1 = 1$, I have made a concrete
assertion having to do
with construction or fusion.

Observe, now, that on certain occasions
$1 + 1 \rightarrow 0$. The formula
$1 + x = 0$, where x
may equal, for instance, $e^{\pi i}$,
may then be of more interest.

Consider, further, $1 = 0$.
This, in mathematical terms, may be called
cancellation. It differs from $0 = 1$,
which may, in mathematical terms, be called
the creation *ex nihil* of number, or,

in non-mathematical terms, the invention
of terror.
Consider, therefore, 0 not equal
to 0, or $0 = x$, where x
is not equal to zero. Climb left through the zero

and watch, looking back at
the blood in its jacket,
the breath in its jacket,
the absence
opening its arms.

ANECDOTE OF THE SQUID

The squid is in fact
a carnivorous pocket
containing a pen, which serves
the squid as his skeleton.

The squid is a raised finger or
an opposed thumb. The squid's quill
is his long, scrupulous nail, which
is invisible.

The squid is a short-beaked
bird who has eaten
his single wing, or impaled
himself on his feather.

The squid, however,
despite his Cadurcian
wineskin and four hundred cups,
does not entertain.

The squid, with his eight
arms and his two
brushes and his sepia,
does not draw.

The squid knows too that the use
of pen and ink is neither recording
impressions nor signing his name
to forms and petitions.

But the squid may be said,
for instance, to transcribe
his silence into the space
between seafloor and wave,

or to invoke an unspoken
word, whose muscular
non-pronunciation the squid
alone is known to have mastered.

The squid carries his ink
in a sack, not a bottle.
With it the squid makes
artifacts.

These are mistakable for
portraiture, or
for self-portraiture, or,
to the eyes of the squid-eating whale,

for the squid, who in the meanwhile grows
transparent and withdraws,
leaving behind him his
coagulating shadows.

Deuteronomy

*And concerning Jehoiakim king of Judah
you shall say, "Thus says the Lord:* You
have burned this scroll. . . . "

Jeremiah XXXVI

AN AUGURY

The raven preceded the dove
out of the ark and for seven days circled
water, waiting for a perch, and for seven more
circled, waiting for the dove.

ESSAY ON ADAM

There are five possibilities. One: Adam fell.
Two: he was pushed. Three: he jumped. Four:
he only looked over the edge, and one look silenced him.
Five: nothing worth mentioning happened to Adam.

The first, that he fell, is too simple. The fourth,
fear, we have tried and found useless. The fifth,
nothing happened, is dull. The choice is between:
he jumped or was pushed. And the difference between these

is only an issue of whether the demons
work from the inside out or from the outside
in: the one
theological question.

DEUTERONOMY

The bush. Yes. It burned like they say it did,
lit up like an oak in October – except
that there is no October in Egypt. Voices
came at me and told me to take off my shoes
and I did that. That desert is full of men's shoes.
And the flame screamed *I am what I am.*
I am whatever it is that is me,
and nothing can but something needs to be
done about it. If anyone
asks, all you can say is, I sent me.

I went, but I brought my brother to do
the talking, and I did the tricks – the Nile
full of fishguts and frogs, the air opaque
and tight as a scab, the white-hot hail,
and boils, and bugs, and when nothing had worked right
we killed them and ran. We robbed them of every
goddamned thing we could get at and carry
and took off, and got through the marsh at low tide
with the wind right, and into the desert. The animals
died, of course, but we kept moving.

Abraham came up easy. We took
the unknown road and ate hoarfrost and used
a volcano for a compass. I had no plan.
We went toward the mountains. I wanted, always,
to die in the mountains, not in that delta.
And not in a boat, at night, in swollen water.
We travelled over dead rock and drank dead water,
and the hoarfrost wasn't exactly hoarfrost.
They claimed it tasted like coriander,
but no two men are agreed on the taste
of coriander. Anyway,
we ate it, and from time to time we caught quail.

Men and half-men and women, we marched
and plodded into those hills, and they exploded
into labyrinths of slag. The air licked us
like a hot tongue, twisting and flapping and gurgling
through the smoke like men suffocating or drowning, saying
An eye for an eye, and on certain occasions
two eyes for one eye. Either way, you model me
in thin air or unwritten words, not in wood,
not in metal. I am gone from the metal when the metal
hits the mold. You will not get me into any image
which will not move when I move, and move
with my fluency. Moses! Come up!

I went, but I wore my shoes and took a waterskin.
I climbed all day, with the dust eating holes
in my coat, and choking me, and the rock cooking me.
What I found was a couple of flat stones
marked up as if the mountain had written all over them.
I was up there a week, working to cool them,
hungry and sweating and unable to make sense of them,
and I fell coming down and broke both of them.
Topping it all, I found everybody down there drooling
over Aaron's cheap figurines, and Aaron chortling.

I went up again to get new stones
and the voices took after me that time and threw me
up between the rocks and said I could see them.
They were right. I could see them. I was standing right
          behind them
and I saw them. I saw the mask's insides,
and what I saw is what I have always seen.
I saw the fire and it flowed and it was moving away
and not up into me. I saw nothing
and it was widening all the way around me.
I collected two flat stones and I cut them
so they said what it seemed to me two stones
should say, and I brought them down without dropping them.

The blisters must have doubled my size, and Aaron said
I almost glowed in the dark when I got down.
Even so, it seemed I was pulling my stunts
more often then than in Egypt. I had to,
to hold them. They had to be led to new land,
and all of them full of crackpot proverbs and cockeyed
ideas about directions. Aaron and I
outbellowed them day after day and in spite of it
they died. Some of weakness, certainly, but so many of them
died of being strong. The children stood up to it
best, out of knowing no different – but with no
idea what to do with a ploughshare, no
idea what a river is. What could they do
if they got there? What can they even know how to wish for?
I promised them pasture, apple trees, cedar,
waterfalls, snow in the hills, sweetwater
wells instead of these arroyos, wild grapes. . . .

Words. And whatever way I say them, words only.
I no longer know why I say them, even though
the children like hearing them. They come when I call them
and their eyes are bright, but the light in them is empty.
It is too clear. It contains. . . the clarity only.
But they come when I call to them. Once I used to sing them
a song about an eagle and a stone, and each time
I sang it, somehow the song seemed changed
and the words drifted into the sunlight. I do not
remember the song now, but I remember
that I sang it, and the song was the law and the law
was the song. The law is a song, I am certain. . . .
And I climbed to the head of this canyon. They said
I could look down at the new land
if I sat here, and I think it is so, but my eyes
are no longer strong, and I am tired now of looking.

The Old in Their Knowing

A hundred generations, twenty-five centuries ago, in tiny seacoast towns and outports strung through the northern Mediterranean, pinned to the sea's edge by the horned mountains rising close behind, among sailors and farmers and fishermen and potters, lived a scattering of men who knew no distinctions between physicist, philosopher, biologist and poet, and who were, each in his own way, all in one. We call them now the Presocratics. Unlike Socrates, they argued with themselves and not their listeners. Unlike Plato, they were not in business to reorder and convince. Unlike Aristotle, as Aristotle says, they were more interested in the union than the distinction between intellect and feeling.

Some of them wrote in verse, some in what may or may not have been prose. Still others, including Pythagoras, evidently never bothered to write anything. They have in common that their work survives in fragments, if at all. But if it is true that for us the fragment is the atom of the form, this brokenness is one more bond between them and ourselves. In these poems, therefore, there are sometimes passages of plain translation.

They had too much faith in the physical world, Aristotle says, and that is why they contradict themselves.

They saw moreover that the whole physical world was in motion, with nothing coming true from its continuous transformation, and they decided that nothing at all could be truthfully said about something that was always and everywhere changing. From these conclusions stem the more extreme views of some who claimed to out-Herakleitos Herakleitos. Take Kratylos for example. Finally he stopped talking altogether and only moved his finger. And he censured Herakleitos for saying one could not step twice into the same river. His own view was that one could not do so even once.

Metaphysics 1010a

HERAKLEITOS

I

Herakleitos says a dry soul is wisest and best.
Herakleitos is undeniably
right in these matters. These
bright tatters of wisdom, cast
over grey welter and spume should at any rate yield
a few visions and reflections, a little light
cutting crosswise like a fin,
splayed against the sea's grain
or annealed on the wave crest.

A dry soul. Dry: that is to say
kiln-dried, cured like good lumber or old Bordeaux,
salt-pork and pemmican, meat of the soul
under the chokecherry,
                              sunlight
and sea-salt arrayed in the grain.

II

Herakleitos says something of concord – not
like a carpenter's clamp or lashed
logs, as in Homer.
Harmony with an arched back,
laminated ash upended like an unlaid keel, the curl
of live flesh in the fire, flexed
like the soul between the muscle and the bone, like
the bow, like the lyre.

III

All things are exchangeable for
fire and fire for all things,
like gold for goods and goods for gold,
or so sings old
                    Herakleitos.

IV

Dead men are gods, men are dead gods, said
Herakleitos. And furthermore,
mortal immortals are immortal mortals,
the breath of the one is the death of the other,
the dying of one is the life of the other:

mortals are deathless, the deathless are mortal,
living in the body the death of the other,
dying into air, earth and fire, siring

the other, the utter
incarnation.

V

Wind stirs his ashes.

PARMENIDES

for J. Michael Yates

Parmenides was no fool. Parmenides
knew that the coast of Campania
wasn't the Aegean's east rim,
that it wasn't Phokaia,
and the rich holes of Calabria,
regardless Pythagoras,
were dust-bins in comparison
to Miletus.

Larger: yes: to be sure.
The great frontier, and the Tyrrhene waves were
strangely like Texas,
and the sheer
size of it all may have got to him.

Parmenides talked
and Parmenides was capable of observing
that his voice drained off under the outsized rocks
and his dreams were pale
like pyrites, or paler, like the gangue
milled away from Ionian metal.

Thirty-odd years, and thirty lines wasted
on wagonaxles, doorhinges, horses, veils
and the sun's girls, and suddenly
then
Parmenides
hummed to himself, caught an idea clean
in his teeth and bit into it, singing:

  . . . things which appear to be,
even though they all exist, actually

have to be there
always. Everywhere.

And Parmenides lay in the goat-dunged heavy-stemmed
grass, imagining things and thinking
of all of them *there* in the inwoven ply, his mind flying
and gulping, trying for the whole cascade:
his brainlobes pumping like lungs, like a muscle,
the nervecords thundering in the bones' coulisses
and the heart's whole cargo coming
tumbling up into him:
goddesses, girls, white water, olive trees,
sharks' roe, the sea-haze,
the migrating eye of the flounder

. . . have to be there
always. Everywhere.

And this revelation
distressed and dumbfounded
Parmenides.
Nevertheless he pushed into it,
choked on exhaustion, swallowed, piled into it:
the whole bill of lading,
everything intermingling into

finally, only
the endless, full,
indivisible stillness:
the lock
on the safe of creation.

Parmenides then took up law
and wrote numerous statutes,
a very great number of statutes
which, Plutarch reports,
were enforced for some years in Elea.

MILETOS

One looked down and the other looked around
when Anaximander and Anaximenes
learned their master Thales
had been drowned.

A SHORT HISTORY

"And he talks of time," said Hippolytus,
the fat-headed presbyter,
of Anaximander, Milesian
sage, then nine centuries dead.

What Anaximander in fact says is:
the necessity is
that things flare out into that out of which
they came to be, because

they pay one another the penalty
and compensation for
the mutual injustice of their
chronological order.

Anaximander does not talk of time.
He lays open the way for
Anaximenes' love of the live air
as a bluer arcanum.

EMPEDOKLES: SEVEN FRAGMENTS

I

Maxillae went into motion without mandibles,
arms walked naked, unhinged from their shoulders,
eyeballs wandered without brows. . . .

II

A lot of them sprouted sternums and eyes on both sides.
Ungulates with human faces, also the opposite,
ox-headed bipeds appeared. Other mixtures: creatures
part man and part woman, with umbrous broadleaf limbs.

III

This is how the fire, as it separated, germinated
the night-flowering seedlings of human beings. Listen.
The lesson is relevant and full of information. Listen.
Crooked forms imprinted out of earth existed first. They
were partly water and partly opaque shape. Fire
desired to arrive at its own image, therefore fire
forced them into flower. They didn't yet have attractive limbs,
nor the hand and the lonely voice which fuse in a man.

IV

. . . tumbling in the surf and undertow
of blood, where the thing called thought is. Thought
is, in fact, the blood around the beating heart.

V

. . . sighting in on the peaks, one after the other, and not just
talking one straight trail through the understory words.

VI

There is an instrument of mandamus, an edict issued
long ago by the gods. It does not expire. It is sealed
edge to edge with promises. It says that whenever
one of the demons who are doomed to immortality hexes
his hands, commits a murder or perjury, he is to be
banished for three hundred centuries. He is to be born
into mortal bodies, exiled from happiness, inhabiting
one incarnation of pain after another. The high air
hounds him into the sea and the sea deposits him
in the dirt, which heaves him into the sunlight and the sunlight
drives him back into the undertow of air. Each takes him
from the other but none of them offers him shelter.
I am one of these, a vagrant, a refugee from gods.
Me. I believe in a drunken brawl.

VII

They come among the animals as mountain cats
and among the broadleaf trees in the forms of laurels.

EMPEDOKLES' RECIPES

Blood and muscle: roughly equal
quantities of storm, earth,
fire, and the high clear air
as they came together in lagoons.

Bone: made in caverns out of
two parts earth, two parts gleaming
hunger, and four parts fire.

The commentators say that Empedokles'
hunger is nothing but water.
And the commentators say
Empedokles' last formula was for

mind: made in volcanoes
out of cauterized eyes and vaporized
muscle, blood and bone.

PHEREKYDES

Pherekydes, in summary, thus: *In the beginning*
were time, earth, and the god.
And the tissue of being

was woven by the god and given as a marriage gift
on the marriage of the underground and the god:
the embroidered surface of the world

thrown over the treeroots' wingspread, over the nakedness
of gods; and the thread-ends
swept out and forgotten.

All things thereafter have been born
in the belly of the earth, in the seven
valleys, out of the seven inland streams.

Or a god put a veil on the ugly mud
and married it, and Pherekydes'
dust, when he was buried, sifted home.

There remains of the mind of Pherekydes:
the esker and the glacial milk,
the high spring runoff in the gorge,

and the waterfalls hammered out of cloud
against the mid cliff,
vanishing in the hungry Himalayan air.

PYTHAGORAS

lemuribus vertebratis, ossibus inter tenebras

I

Remnants: the thirty-nine rules, a sundial
untied like a shoelace, a theory of number
dismembered and scattered like dice. And the third-hand
chatter over the transmigrations of souls.
And a story: Pythagoras wouldn't eat meat
and his legs buckled under him.
                                    Rubble
of picked-over thought, broken pediments, cracked
roof-tiles laid up with mortar now gone in the rain.

Seabirds over the high grass,
nothing erect
except these pillars:
the mind of Pythagoras stands on two columns of words.

II

Not the calculus. Numbers. Integers
tethered into crystal-structures: copper, antimony. . . .
Integers driven like nails into inflexible void.

Dull-eyed disciples, centuries later, sitting
down to count the catalog,
mumbling over multipliers.

III

Unity is a substance, not a property. Light
is finite and motionless. Darkness
is the everlasting verb.

Strangeness is four-square.
Plurality curves
and the darkness is plural.
And only the left hand moves.

And the darkness... this... *these*
darknesses are everywhere.

The sundial's tooth is the token,
like a carpenter's rule. The sharpened
darkness is simply the index.
Light
does not move, and light is the tool.

IV

The principle, therefore:
transparency.

Shaving the obsidian
to the clarity of the clean talon;
leaving no furrow or footprint or stripped stem,
no trace of rest between two intervals of motion;
the tongue to cast no shadow
on the word, the hand no shadow on the stone.

Darkness arcs over the head, said Pythagoras.
Forget the head. Paint portraits of the mind.
Darkness flows between closed fingers.
Draw me the god without the body. Only
the intangible tangency, sculpture like the plucked string
and speech on the model of inaudible singing.
The plane is tuned by tightening the line.

V

Octaves of silence
do not exist and do not echo. Intervals
of darkness disassemble
endlessly. *Do not drink*
the darkness, said Pythagoras,
the soul cannot become pure darkness.
Possibly. Possibly.

DEMOKRITOS

I

Bearing children is even more dangerous,
said Demokritos, than buying a mirror,
yet this wealth strangely easy to come by –
a bed and two books,
bread and fruit and a strong pair of shoes.
In spite of bad government there was good weather,
but after the heart the first thing
to sour is always the water.
The demon's summerhouse is the soul.

II

What is is no more than what isn't;
the is, no advance on the isn't. Is
is isn't with rhythm.
Touching and turning the isn't is is.
Not being is basic. As silence is,
isn't is – during, before and after the sound.
Isn't is everywhere. In you. Outside.
Presence is absence keeping time.

III

That which splits off from the edgeless has edges.
It dries into light, it ignites into fire.
Fire and mind I believe to be
round, though knowledge is always
lopsided, like elm leaves.
Nose, eyes, ears, tongue
and fingers are fingers – all fingers
groping for imprints in the intermittent air.

IV

Such giants we are and so hardly
here, mere shapes in the dust and our
deaf hands yelling so loud,
the diaphanous blood, the diaphanous
bone, and the truth so small as it crumbles it swims
in and out of the intestine,
floats through the ear's net, the eye's net,
the sieve of the palm.

V

A man must be ready for death
always, as sound must always be ready
for silence. There are of course contrary yearnings,
called information and music, but call it
laughter or call it
beatitude, a good joke is the most you can ask.

VI

The uncountable rhythms uncountable
worlds – more in some places than others.
Motion, on closer inspection, appears
to be limited to reverberation and falling.
Never look down without turning.
Never live with your back to the mountains.
Never mend net with your back to the sea.

VII

Thus the earth goes south each summer.
The mind moults in the north like a widgeon
and rises, hunting or grazing, in autumn,
riding the gale,
the stain of the voice like a handprint at intervals
in the unravelling rigging.

VIII

Incidentally, you may notice,
said Demokritos,
the eagle has black bones.

XENOPHANES

Earth is the ultimate substance.
What is, is made out of earth. We
who climb free of it,
milkthistles, mallards and men,
are made out of earth which is driven by water.

I have found chiton shells high
in the mountains, the finprints of fish
in the stonecutter's stone, and seen
boulders and trees dragged to sea
by the river. Water and earth
lurch, wrestle and twist in their purposeless
war, of which we
are a consequence, not an answer.

*

The earth gives birth to the sun
each morning, and washes herself in the water,
and slits the sun's throat every night
with a splintered stone, and washes
herself once again in the water.

Some days the sun, like a fattening
goose, crosses over in ignorant stupor.
Other days, watch: you will see him
shudder and twitch, like a rabbit
caught in the snare – but what
does it matter? One way
or the other, his death is the same.

We must learn to be thought
by the gods, not to think them.
Not to think gods have two eyes and ten fingers,

thirty-two teeth and two
asymmetrical footprints. Not to think
here in the unstoppered bowls
of our skulls we hold luminous
godbreath. The mush in our skulls
is compiled, like our toenails,
of rocksalt and silt, which is matted
like felt in the one case, and swollen
like hope in the other:

What is, is earth. What dies
is earth driven by water.

*

The earth has one end. It is under
our feet. You may think
differently; I am convinced
there is no other.

OF THE SNARING OF BIRDS

from the Antigone *of Sophocles, a version*
in memory of Martin Heidegger, 1889 – 1977

Strangeness is frequent enough, but nothing
is ever as strange as a man is.
For instance
out there,
riding the grey-maned water,
heavy weather on the southwest quarter,
jarred by the sea's thunder,
tacking through the bruise-blue waves.
Or he paws at the eldest of goddesses,
earth, as though she were made
out of gifts and forgiveness,
driving his plough in its circle year after year
with what used to be horses.

Birds' minds climb the air, yet he snares them,
and creatures of the field.
These
and the flocks
of the deep sea. He unfurls
his folded nets for their funeral shrouds.
Man the tactician.
See, by his sly
inventions he masters
his betters – the deep-throated
goats of the mountain,
and horses. His yokes ride the necks
of the tireless bulls who once haunted these hills.

And the sounds in his own throat
gather the breezes that rise in his mind.
He has learned how to sit on committees,
and learned to build houses and barns
against blizzards and gales.
He manages all and yet manages
nothing. Nothing is closed
to the reach of his will,
and yet he has found no road out of hell.
His fate, we all say, is precisely
what he has never outwitted.

Wise, yes – or ingenious.
More knowledge than hope in his hand,
and evil comes out of it sometimes,
and sometimes he creeps toward nobility.
Warped on the earth's loom
and dyed in the thought of the gods,
a man should stand high in his city.
But he is no citizen whatsoever
if he is tied to the ugly by love of adventure.
May no one who will not wonder what he is and does
suddenly arrive at my fireside.

THE PETELIA TABLET

*(Inscription on gold foil, from a tomb in southern Italy,
perhaps fourth century* B.C.)

You will come to a well on the left side of hell's house.
A white cypress stands by it, luminous, pale.
Stay clear of this well at all cost. Don't drink from this well.
You will come to another, where cold water flows
from the marshes of memory. Sentinels stand there.
Say: *I am earth's and the starred sky's child, but the sky's
blood runs in my veins; you can see this yourselves.
Thirst withers me. Hurry, give me
the cold water flowing from the lake of memory.*
They will give you water from the sacred wellhead,
and you will be known .   .   .   .   heroes from then on.
.   .   .   .   going to die
.   .   .   .   .   .   this writing .   .   .   .   .   .
.   .   .   .   the darkness closing over.

Hachadura

La Hachadura, "Hard Axe," is the name of a village in Ahuachapán, El Salvador, to which this poem bears in my own mind certain tonal and temporal affiliations. The piece is offered, however, as music, not as cartography. For listening; not, like a map or a roadsign, for reading. If it is any good of its kind, it is proof against sectarian interpretations, including those advanced by its author. Still, the best editor I have ever had, and am ever likely to have, has prodded me relentlessly to introduce it.

One expects to find in a piece of absolute music the development of themes, not the progress of an argument – and the themes here must be obvious enough. They include, for instance, the theme that negation is basic: that we protrude into the nothingness, as Heidegger says – and, as Demokritos says, that it protrudes into us. They include also that story left us by the ancients, of a man too long away: a man who cannot go home any more than a circle can touch its center, and who is nonetheless determined to return. They include the theme of the sisterhood of life and non-life, even of non-life and divinity, and the theme of the death without and within us, the weaponry integral to us, which makes a true disarmament seem impossible. Death, our teeth and bones remind us, is departure and return.

If I have named the poem correctly, these themes have something to do with the ruined landscape of El Salvador as I knew it, years ago, before the present guerrilla war. La Hachadura, when I saw it last, was a simple church reeking of crucifixion, with some satellite huts and houses sheltering hungry people in a deforested, sunleached land. A little ways distant was, and is, a military prison as infamous as any in the hemisphere.

There, in that desecrated country called The Savior, salvation – if that means crawling out from under the rock of history – seemed more impossible than ever. And there, where the cultures of the old and new worlds have mingled as thoroughly as anywhere, even the simplest forms of human harmony seemed hopeless to maintain.

I thought, when I composed this piece, that the moral weather in El Salvador had nothing local about it: that it had gathered out of a heritage (exemplified by the European rape of the Americas), a condition (ignorance, hunger, despair) and a biology (soft flesh and sharp talons) which belong acutely to us all. These several years later, the torture chambers are fuller, the tree cover is scarcer, the hungry are more numerous, and I see no reason to change my mind.

I do not, of course, pretend to have made anything equal to the speechlessness of the dead or the wordlessness of the dying in that country, nor even to have made a work in which those voices can be heard. This is not a poem *about* El Salvador, however much I ought to have written one. Yet I think it has something to do with our uncanny ability to recreate El Salvador on continent after continent, century after century, time after time.

How can a man make music in the face of these preoccupations? A durable question. How, given the chance, can he do otherwise?

Many of the motives, though none of the themes, are filched from a very different and apparently joyful work by Wallace Stevens. The purpose of this theft, if it was not mere covetousness and venality, was, I suppose, to test the structural analogy to music – for the poem has, if I am not mistaken, no narrative, no program, any more than Bartók's First Piano Concerto or one of John Lewis's jazz fugues has a program. It is a chaconne for solo intelligence in twelve fragments.

What, nevertheless, it is fair to ask, does the ghost of Wallace Stevens, in his comfortable apartments, have to do with the bitter fate of human beings in a village in Ahuachapán? *Lend no part to any humanity that suffuses / you in its own light,* he counselled himself one day. And on the same page, addressing the words themselves and the universe:

> *Shine alone, shine nakedly, shine like bronze,*
> *that reflects neither my face nor any inner part*
> *of my being, shine like fire, that mirrors nothing.*

I

There is a nothing like the razor
edge of air, another

like the tongued pebbles, syllables
of sea-wind and sea-color and

another and another like the salt
hide drying inward, eating

in through the underbelly of the bone,
the grain

of the sea-eaten iron, and the open
lattice of the wave.

There is the nothing, moreover,
at which Eurytos never
quite arrives, tallying
the dust with the four-finger
abacus
unsheathed from the flesh of his hand.

Suppose, therefore, a certain
concretion of order,
unstable or at any rate in motion, but a certain
concretion of order inherent in one
of the innumerable
forms of such a number. Therefore:

darkness under the sunrise,
darkness in the hollow of the hand;

inside the spine the darkness, the darkness
simmering in the glands;

the rumpled blade of darkness which is
lodged in every fissure of the brain;

the membrane
of the darkness which is always

interposed
between two surfaces when they close.

II

The bird is the color of gunmetal
in sunlight, but it is midnight;
the bird the color of gunmetal
in sunlight is flying
under the moon.

There is a point at which
meridians are knotted
into nothing and a region
into which meridians fray and intertwine,
but not like mooring lines; they
fray like the leading and trailing edges
of wings, running from nothingness
to muscle and strung from the muscle back again.

Listen: the sounds are the sounds of meridians
trilling, meridians drawn to produce
the illusion of plectrum, tuning pegs and a frame,
or perhaps to produce Elijah's
audition: the hide
of the silence curing,
tanning,
tightening into the wind.

Or the sounds are the sounds of the air opening
up over the beak and closing over the vane,
opening over the unmoving cargo slung
between the spine and the talon,
slung between the wingbone and the brain.

III

It is for nothing, yes,
this manicuring, barbering, this
shaving of the blade.

Nothing: that is that the edge should come
to nothing as continuously
and cleanly and completely as it can.

And the instruction
is given, therefore,
to the archer, sharpening

the blood and straightening
the vein: the same instruction
that is given to the harper:

Tap.
Strum the muscle.
Breathe.

And come to nothing.

IV

Consider the magnetism of bone,
the blood-magnetic
fleshfield eddying in
and out of the marrow
under the blood-flux in the vein.

The apple is the palpable
aura and hysteresis
of the seed, the tissue is
a proof of the polarity and necessary
coldness of the bone.

V

In the high West there is everything
it is that the high West consists of,
mountains,
named animals and unnamed birds,

mountain water, mountain trees
and mosses, and the marrow of the air
inside its luminous blue bone.
And the light that lies just under darkness,
Artemis

grazing the ice
that is sea-rose under the sunset, and sea-green
and sea-deep under the snow's froth. Under
the still white water the sudden
fissure in the wave.

Measure from the surface,
measure from the light's edge
to the surface of the darkness, measure
from the light's edge to the sound.

VI

My Connecticut uncle stares into his manicured
thumbnail, thinking of his Riviera uncle's
smoked-glass monocle. A one-eyed sun-goggle,
halfway useful in the lethal roselight. Notice
nevertheless it seems the light drills
up the nerve backward, welling underneath
the retina and altering the eye's aim. Notice
that the colored cores of the air lurch up
the ear, blue-gold and maroon against the blind drum.
Notice in addition the others at this intersection:
this one who is talking, this one who is standing
in the shoes of the man who is wearing them and sitting,
this one with, undeniably, a knife in his hand,
this one, this one saying nothing. . . .

VII

Empedokles says the talon
is the crystallization
of the tendon, the nail is the wintered nerve.
Or the antler is the arrowhead
of the arrow threading the axeheads of the spine.

The Aristotelian then
wonders whether leather stands
in similar relation
to the muscle, and if sunlight might
be said to shed the darkness back of the stone.

VIII

The mules the angels ride come slowly down
the blazing passes, over the high scree
and the relict ice, through the lichen-spattered
boulders and the stunted timber. Slowly

but as noiselessly as is
proper to the progeny of sea-mares
and celestial asses. Down
through the gentian and the peppergrass, down
through the understory dark

between these trees, down through the recurved waves
and into unlightable water. The mules
the angels ride go to summer pasture
somewhere on the seafloor or still deeper.

IX

Chitin and calcareous accretions
no longer clothe me. Meat
has eaten the fossil;
the body is no longer able
to moult the bone.

Or as the field notes
show for August:
the squid has swallowed the quill; the animal
has successfully attempted
to incarcerate the cage.

X

The bud of light before the sunrise
mated with the dusk,
bore rock and jagged water,
mated with the water, bore
the tidal bore, the overfall, the spindrift and the mist.

The starlight seeded earth and mist and water,
germinating slime.
Slime ate into the rocksalt and the darkness,
the seacrust and the metamorphic stone, breeding
nail and nervecord, bone marrow, molar and

bones taking root in the darknesses
and darknesses
flowering out of the bone.
Gods and men and goddesses
and ghosts are grown out of this,

brothers of the bark and the heartwood and the thorn,
brothers of the gull and the staghorn coral,
brothers of the streptococcus,
the spirochete, the tiger, the albatross, the sea-spider,
cousins of lime and nitrogen and rain.

XI

In the blood's alluvium
there are alphabets: feldspars and ores,
silt jamming the mouths, and the sea's weight
or the white magmatic fire
is required to read the spoor:

the thumbprint on the air, the soul's print
beached on the foreshore under the slag,
the spine-tracks and excavations
of sea urchins
climbing the high crags.

XII

These, therefore, are the four
ages of man:
pitch-black, blood-color, piss-color, colorless.

After the season of iron the season
of concrete and tungsten alloy and plastic,
and after the season of concrete the season
of horn, born in the black October,

hooves and feathers hooves and feathers
shudder past the tusks
and navigate back between the horns.

Jacob Singing

for Roo Borson & Joseph Keller

Jacob. His name means He Follows, He Climbs, He Succeeds, and now in the hills near the Gulf of Suez his name means simply Mountain Quail. He was the craftier and the smoother and by a few moments also the younger of twin brothers. With the help of his mother, Rebekah, he dressed one day in the hide of a freshly slaughtered goat and went into the tent of his blind father, Isaac. The masquerade was successful. He received there the blessing meant for his hairier twin named Esau, who was at that moment out hunting.

Within days of this fraud, Jacob left the country. On the way out he slept in the open, as everyone knows, with a stone for a pillow, and during the night his eyes wove ladders reaching the stars. On his return many years later, as everyone also knows, he wrestled all night with an angel who finally, at sunrise, crippled him and traded him names.

His sons were Joseph and Benjamin, Reuben, Simeon, Levi, and seven others – the fathers of the twelve tribes of Israel. Of these his favorite, Joseph, of the coat of many colors, was sold into slavery by his jealous elder brothers.

When Jacob too was old, and his eyesight was gone, he was taken by wagon to Egypt and there at last reunited with Joseph. The Book of Genesis tells us how, during this reunion, Joseph brought in his two sons, Jacob's grandsons, and how the old man reached out, left over right, to bless them, crossing his arms. Ephraim and Manasseh are the grandsons, and Jacob is called by his new name, Israel:

And Joseph took them both, Ephraim in his right hand toward Israel's left hand, and Manasseh in his left hand toward Israel's right hand, and brought them near unto him. And Israel stretched out his right hand and laid it upon Ephraim's head, who was the younger, and his left hand upon Manasseh's head, guiding his hands willingly. . . . And Joseph said unto his father, Not so, my father: for this is the firstborn; put thy right hand upon his head. And his father refused, and said, I know it, my son, I know it: he also. . . .

And the Lord thy God shall circumcise thine heart, and the heart of thy seed. . . .

Genesis XLVIII / Deuteronomy XXX

What I am I have stolen.
I have climbed the mountain with nothing in my hand
except the mountain. I have spoken to the god
with nothing in my hand except my other hand.
One against the other, the smith against the wizard,
I have watched them. I have watched them
wrestle one another to the ground.
I have watched my body carry my head around
like a lamp, looking for light among the broken stones.

What I am I have stolen.
Even the ingrained web
in the outstretched palm of this body,
limping on oracle finger and thumb,
dragging a great weight, an arm or a tail
like the wake of a boat drug over the ground.
What I am I have stolen. Even my name.

My brother, I would touch you but these
are your hands. Yours, yours, though I call them
my own. My brother, I would hold your shoulders
but only the voice is mine. My brother,
the head is a hand that does not open
and the face is full of claws.

What I am I have stolen.
These mountains which were never mine
year after year have remade me.
I have seen the sky colored with laughter.
I have seen the rocks between the withered water
and the quaking light. I have climbed the mountain
with nothing in my hand except the handholds
as I came upon them, leaving my hands behind.

I have eaten the sun, it is my muscle,
eaten the moon, it is my bone.

I have listened to the wind, whipped
in the heart's cup, slap and whistle in the vein.

My father said:
the wood will crawl into the apple,
the root will crawl into the petal,
the limb will crawl into the sepal
and hide.
But the fruit has eaten the tree, has eaten the flower.
The body which is flower and fruit together
has swallowed its mother, root and stem.
The lungs are leaves and mine are golden.

I have seen the crow carry the moon
against the mountain.
I have seen the sky crawl under a stone.

I have seen my daughter
carried on the land's shoulder.
I have seen the wind change
color above her.
I have lain in silence, my mouth to the ground.

I have seen the light drop
like a wagon-sprag in the crisp stubble.
I have seen the moon's wheels
bounce through the frozen ruts
and chirp against the pebbles.
I have seen the metal angels
clatter up and down.

I have seen the flushed ewes
churn in the pen and the picked rams boil
against the hazel. I have seen them
strip the poplar, scrub the buckeye bare.
I have seen the mixed flocks
flow through the scented hills like braided oil.
I who never moved as they do.

I have climbed the mountain
one foot up and one hoof down.

The breath is a bone the flesh comes loose around.

Flower and fruit together.
But this other, this other
who is always in the body,
his lungs in the belly and
his head between the thighs.
O his arms go backward,
his legs go side to side.

My son, you have asked for a blessing. I give you
this blessing. I tell you,

the eye will flow out of the socket like water,
the ear will gore like a horn
and the tongue like another,
the sailor will stay in his house near the harbor,
the laborer, blinkered and fed, will stay at his labor,
the soldier will soldier,
the lawyer will smile like milk and swill liquor,
the judge will glide like a snake keeping pace with the horses,
the man with gay eyes will like chocolate,
the roebuck will wrestle the air and you will hear music,
the rancher will prosper,
the wolf will walk out of your hand and his teeth will
        be shining.

But this one, my grandson, the young one,
this one will steal the eye and the tooth
of the mountain. This one will ride with his dogs
through the galleries of vision. This one will move
among the rain-worn shapes of men
with faces in his hands and the fingers writhing.
This one will slide his spade through the sea
and come away carrying wheat and linen.

This one, the young one, will steal
the sun and the moon,
the eye and the tooth of the mountain.
This one, the young one, how tall,
shaking hands and trading armor
with his dark-eyed brother.

My son, you must do more
than listen to the angel; you must wrestle him.
And one thing further: he must be there.
The muscle in the air, the taut light
hinged in the milky gristle
and the swollen dark, the smell
like the smell of a cornered animal.

I have oiled these stones to sharpen the wind.
I have come or I have gone, I have forgotten.
I hold what I hold
in this chiasma of the hands.

I have set my ear against the stone
and heard it twirling.
I have set my teeth against the stone
and someone said he heard it singing.

The Stonecutter's Horses

This is in some measure the story of Francesco Petrarca, who was a gentleman, and a scholar, and a brilliant poet, and a good Roman Catholic, and the father of an illegitimate daughter whom he loved very deeply and whose illegitimacy was, for him, a source of incurable pain. His feelings concerning himself and his daughter grew so intense that for years he would not speak her name in public, though he pronounced it often enough and lovingly enough in private. After her marriage he sought to simplify his affairs and his explanations by adopting as his foster son the man he might have called his son-in-law: his daughter's husband Brossano. With him and few others, Petrarca shared the story of his precious wound.

On the morning of 4 April 1370, in one of the upper rooms of his house in Padova, in the north of Italy, Francesco Petrarca summoned his secretary, to whom he dictated in simple Italian the first draft of his last will and testament. A later version of this document – the dry and guarded Latin rewrite which Petrarca considered suitable for public disclosure – still survives. Only an occasional flash in the Latin suggests the rough glint of its predecessor. The close, for instance, reads: *Ego Franciscus Petrarca scripsi qui testamentum aliud fecissem si essem dives ut vulgus insanem putat.* "I, Francesco Petrarca, have written this. I would have made a different testament if I were rich, as the lunatic public believes me to be." The Italian original would, I believe, have begun with a meditative wail: *Io, Francesco, io, io. . . .*

I, Francesco, this April day:
death stirs like a bud in the sunlight, and Urban
has got off his French duff and re-entered Rome
and for three years running has invited me to Rome,
over the bright hills and down the Cassia,
back through Arezzo one more time,
my age sixty-five and my birthday approaching,
the muggers on the streets in broad daylight in Rome,
the hawks and the buzzards. . . .
                              Take this down.

No one has thought too deeply of death.
So few have left anything toward or against it.
Peculiar, since thinking of death can never be
wasted thinking, nor can it be come to
too quickly. A man carries his death with him
everywhere, waiting, but seldom thinking
of waiting. Death is uncommonly like the soul.

What I own other than that ought to fall
of its own weight and settle. But beggars and tycoons
and I are concerned with our possessions,
and a man with a reputation for truth
must have one also for precision.
                              I leave
my soul to my saviour, my corpse to the earth.
And let it be done without any parades.
I don't care very much where I'm buried,
so it please God and whoever is digging.
Still, you will ask. You will badger me.
If I am dead you will badger each other.
But don't lug my bones through the public streets
in a box to be gabbled at and gawked at and followed.
Let it be done without any parades.

If I die here in Padova, bury me here
near the friend who is dead who invited me here.
If I die on my farm, you can use the chapel
I mean to build there, if I ever build it.
If not, try the village down the road.

If in Venezia, near the doorway.
If in Milano, next to the wall.
In Pavia, anywhere. Or if in Rome...
if in Rome, in the center, of course, if there's room.
These are the places I think I might die in
in Italy.
        Or if I happen to be in Parma,
there is a cathedral of which, for some reason,
I am the archdeacon. But I will avoid
going to Parma. It would scarcely be possible,
I suppose, in Parma, not to have a parade.

At any rate, put what flesh I have left
in a church. A Franciscan church if there is one.
I don't want it feeding a tree from which
rich people's children swipe apples.

Two hundred ducats go to the church in which
I am buried, with another hundred to be given
out in that parish to the poor, in small doses.
The money to the church, let it buy a piece of land
and the land be rented and the rental from the land
pay for an annual mass in my name.
I will be fitter company in that sanctuary
then, present in spirit and name only,
than this way, muttering to the blessed virgin
through my hemorrhoids and bad teeth. I should be glad
to be rid of this sagging carcass.
                  Don't write that.

I have cleared no fields of their stones. I have built
no barns and no castles. I have built a name

96

out of other men's voices by banging my own
like a kitchen pan. My name to the Church
with the money it takes to have it embalmed.
Very few other things. My Giotto to the Duke.
Most men cannot fathom its beauty. Those
who know painting are stunned by it. The Duke
does not need another Giotto, but the Duke knows painting.

To Dondi, money for a plain ring to remind him
to read me.
                    To Donato – what? I forgive him
the loan of whatever he owes me. And I
myself am in debt to della Seta. Let it
be paid if I haven't paid it. And give him
my silver cup. Della Seta drinks
water. Damned metal ruins the wine.

To Boccaccio, I am unworthy to leave
anything, and have nothing worthy to leave.
Money then, for a coat to keep himself warm
when he works after dark, as he frequently does,
while the river wind stutters and bleats at his window,
and his hand-me-down cordwood fizzles and steams.

My lute to Tommaso. I hope he will play it
for God and himself and not to gain fame
for his playing.
                    These are such trivial legacies.

Money to Pancaldo, but not for the card table.
Money to Zilio – at least his back salary.
Money to the other servants. Money to the cook.
Money to their heirs if they die before I do.

Give my Bible back to the Church.
                    And my horses...

my horses.

        Let a few of my friends, if they wish to,
draw lots for my horses. Horses
are horses. They cannot be given away.

The rest to my heir and executor, Brossano,
who knows he is to split it, and how he is to split it,
and the names I prefer not to put into this
instrument. Names of no other importance.
Care for them. Care for them here in this house
if you can. And don't sell off the land to get money
in any case. Selling the earth without cause
from the soul is simony, Brossano. Real-estate
hucksters are worse than funeral parades.
I have lived long enough in quite enough
cities, notwithstanding the gifts
of free lodging in some of them, long enough, Brossano,
to know the breath moves underfoot in the clay.
The stone quarried and cut and reset
in the earth is a lover's embrace, not an overlay.

The heart splits like a chinquapin pod,
spilling its angular seed on the ground.

Though we ride to Rome and back aboard animals,
nothing ever takes root on the move.
I have seen houses and fields bartered
like cargo on shipboard. But nothing takes root
without light in the eye and earth in the hand.

The land is our solitude and our silence.
A man should hoard what little silence
he is given and what little solitude he can get.

Just the one piece over the mountains
ought, I think, to be given away. Everything
I have ever done that has lasted began there.
And I think my heir will have no need to go there.

If Brossano die before I do,
look to della Seta. And for his part let him
look into that cup. He will know my mind.

A man who can write as I can ought not
to talk of such things at such length. Keep this
back if you can. Let the gifts speak
for themselves if you can, small though they are.
But I don't like the thought of what little there is
spilling into the hands of lawyers through lawsuits.
The law is no ritual meant to be practised
in private by scavengers. Law is the celebration
of duty and the ceremony of vengeance. The Duke's
law has nothing to do with my death
or with horses.
                Done.
                        Ask the notaries to come over
precisely at noon. I will rewrite it
and have it to sign by the time they arrive.

Ptahhotep's River

The one whose names are hidden said: . . .
The gods took root from my sweat, but men and women
from my tears.

Coffin Texts, 1130

THE HEART IS OIL

If a man see himself in a dream seeing his face in a mirror,
beware: it means another wife. —Papyrus Chester Beatty III,
British Museum (Thebes, 19th Dynasty)

If a man should dream and should see himself dreaming
a dream seeing himself in a mirror
seeing that the heart is oil riding
the blood, like a lid toward which he is moving,
his bones like a boat and his gut strung up
for a sail in the wind of his breathing,

if this is his eye in the mirror seeing
his eye in the dream seeing himself
in a mirror seeing his eye seeing
himself in a dream in a mirror, his face
reflected in oil which ruffles from time
to time in the wind of his breathing,

the mirror will flow and the heart will set
like glass in the frame of his bones on the wall
of his breathing, his blood thin as paper and silver,
reflecting his face in his heart in a mirror
in a dream where he sees himself seeing
himself in a mirror seeing

that the bones will float and the heart will shatter,
his bones in his throat and his gut stretched tight
as a sail in the wind of his breathing, his blood
full of broken glass and his face like torn paper
seeing himself in the mirror of his heart
that scatters like oil in the mirror of his breathing.

SPELL FOR WHITE SANDALS

The hall is so wide it will hold both hands.
Is there a floor, you will ask, *or where are we?*
Are we anywhere other
than here or where are we so wide?
It will hold both hands.

Lord, your two eyes, your two daughters,
and one – which one was it? – I married.

Lord, I know there is more than one justice.
Lord, I know there is only one room
in these numerous mansions.

Lord, I have turned my hand out
without knowing my purpose.
Lord, I have turned my hand in
without knowing my purpose less often.
Lord, I have turned my hand without knowing
my purpose against other creatures but less often still.

Lord, I do not know my own name.

I have not shrunk the acre, the ounce, or the hour.
I have not halted a god in his motion.
I have not broken the back of the river.
I have not built in the path of the sun.

I am the breath's edge, the mouth of the well
of water and mineral, of sunlight and air.
Perhaps I remember
not one of the names but a few of the letters:

the one who eats shadows
the one who eats air
the one who the dust is
the one who comes home without ever arriving
the one who arrives without pausing
the one whose face is behind him
the one who eats light
the one whose teeth are whiter than water
the one whose palm has no grain and no creases
the one with uncountable voices

Lord, I have turned my hand over and under
and over. I am the wellmouth, the edge of the air,
the shape thrown up to the light
by my shadow – the light's edge, no more.

I come for the names of my feet now.
I come for the names of my feet as they rise
and fall forward. I come for
the names of my feet as they fall.

THE SONG OF PTAHHOTEP

for George Payerle

Good speech is rarer than jade. It is rarer
than greenstone, yet may be found among girls
at the grindstones, found among shepherds
alone in the hills.
I know how a man might speak to his grandson;
I cannot teach him to speak to the young women.

Still, I have seen at the well how the words
tune the heart, how they make one who hears them
a master of hearing. If hearing enters the hearer,
the hearer turns into a listener. Hearing is better
than anything else. It cleanses the will.

I have seen in the hills how the heart chooses.
The fists of the heart hold the gates of the ears.
If a grandson can hear his grandfather's words,
the words decades later
may rise like smoke from his heart
as he waits on a mountain and thinks of old age.

In the cave of the ear, the bones, like stars
at the solstice, sit upright and still,
listening in on the air as the muscle and blood
listen in on the skeleton.
Tongues and breasts of the unseen
creatures of the air
slither over the bones in the toothless
mouths of the ears.
To hear is to honor the sleeping snail
in the winter woodbox back of the forge.

106

You will see the new governor's ears
fill like pockets, his eyes
swell up with the easily seen,
yet his face is a dumped jug. His bones
wrinkle like bent flutes, his heart
sets and triggers like a beggar's hand.
The new governor's words are orderly, clean,
inexhaustible, and cannot be told
one from another, like funerals, like sand.

I have done what I could in my own time in office.
The river rises, the river goes down.
I have seen sunlight nest on the water.
I have seen darkness
puddle like oil in the palm of my hand.

Speak to your grandson by saying,
good speech is rarer than jade, it is rarer
than greenstone, yet may be found among girls
at the grindstones, found among shepherds
alone in the hills.
The heart is an animal. Learn where it leads.
Know its gait as it breaks. Know its range,
how it mates and feeds.
If they shear your heart bald like a goat, the coat
will grow back, though your heart may shudder from cold.
If they skin out your heart,
it will dry in your throat like a fish in the wind.

Speak to your grandson by saying,
my grandson, the caves of the air
glitter with hoofmarks
left by the creatures
you have summoned there.

My grandson, my grandson,
good speech is rarer than jade, it is rarer
than greenstone, yet may be found among girls
at the grindstones, found among shepherds
alone in the hills. The heart is a boat.
If it will not float, if it have no keel,
if it have no ballast, if it have
neither pole nor paddle nor mast,
there is no means by which you can cross.

Speak to your grandson by saying,
my grandson, the wake of the heart
is as wide as the river,
the drift of the heart is as long as the wind
and as strong as the rudder that glides through your hand.

Speak to your grandson by saying,
good speech is rarer than jade, it is rarer
than greenstone, yet may be found among girls
at the grindstones, found among shepherds
alone in the hills.
The fists of the heart as they open and close
on the rope of the blood in the well of the air
smell of the river.
The heart is two feet and the heart is two hands.
The ears of the blood hear it clapping and walking;
the eyes of the bones see the blooded footprints
it leaves in its path.

Speak to your grandson by saying,
my grandson, set your ear
on the heart's path,
kneeling there in honor
of the sleeping snail.

Bone Flute Breathing

. . . that mirrors nothing.

DEATH BY WATER

It was not his face nor any
other face Narcissus saw
in the water. It was the absence there
of faces. It was the deep clear
of the blue pool he kept on coming
back to, and that kept on coming
back to him as he went to it, shipping
out over it October after October
and every afternoon,
walking out of the land-locked summer,
out of the arms of his voice,
walking out of his words.

It was his eye, you might say,
that he saw there, or
the resonance of its color.
Better yet, say it was what
he listened for – the low
whisper of light along the water, not
the racket among the stones.

Li Po too. As we do – though
for the love of hearing
our voices, and for the fear of hearing
our speech in the voices of others come back
from the earth, we speak while we listen and look
down the long blue pools of air coming toward us and say
they make no sound, they
have no faces, they have one another's eyes.

LEDA AND THE SWAN

for George Faludy

Before the black beak reappeared
like a grin from in back of a drained cup,
letting her drop,
she fed at the sideboard of his thighs,
the lank air whitening in the sunrise,
yes. But no, she put on no knowledge
with his power. And it was his power alone
that she saved of him for her daughter.
Not his knowledge.
No.
He was the one who put on knowledge.
He was the one who looked down out of heaven
with a dark croak, knowing more
than he had ever known before,
and knowing he knew it:

knowing the xylophone of her bones,
the lute of her back and the harp of her belly,
the flute of her throat,
woodwinds and drums of her muscles,
knowing the organpipes of her veins;

knowing her as a man knows mountains he has hunted
naked and alone in –
knowing the fruits, the roots and the grasses,
the tastes of the streams
and the depths of the mosses,
knowing as he moves in the darkness he is also
resting at noon in the shade of her blood –
leaving behind him in the sheltered places
glyphs meaning mineral and moonlight and mind
and possession and memory,

112

leaving on the outcrops signs meaning mountain
and sunlight and lust and rest and forgetting.

Yes. And the beak that opened to croak
of his knowing that morning creaked like a re-hung
door and said nothing, felt nothing. The past
is past. What is known is as lean
as the day's edge and runs one direction.
The truth floats
down, out of fuel,
indigestible, like a feather. The lady
herself, though, whether
or not she was truth – or untruth, or both, or was neither –
she dropped through the air like a looped rope,
a necklace of meaning, remembering
everything forwards and backwards,
and lit like a fishing skiff gliding aground.

That evening, of course, while her husband, to whom
she told nothing, strode like the king
of Lakonia through the orchestra
pit of her body, touching
this key and that string in his passing,
she lay like so much
green kindling,
fouled tackle and horseharness under his hands
and said nothing, felt
nothing, but only
lay thinking
not flutes, lutes and xylophones,
no: thinking soldiers
and soldiers and soldiers and soldiers
and daughters,
the rustle of knives in his motionless wings.

THE BETTER MAN

Simple enough. At the sound of him singing
their names, rocks, trees, middle-aged
women and most of the rest of creation
shot straight for his head and collided.

Since then it has been
the custom with musical
children
to put out the eyes.

Sailors and the hill people
buried what they could find of him.
Adolescents, potential
suicides and the wounded

attempted the names.
Safe in each case, as it happened –
like all the others – in their own
pronunciations.

Afterward, too, the explainers
moved through the towns with their versions
and justifications.
They said, for example, the song

was brought on by a woman.
Some of them said that the red-headed
woman who loved him had left
and was dead when he found her.

Others insisted he'd killed her. A third
told a long and haphazard story
in which she had gone on a pilgrimage
down the valley and met, unexpectedly

but quite simply, a better man,
with a liking for conversation
and chess, and a milder
face, and a foreign name.

They said that the death had nothing to do
with shaped light or the sheer
edges of the air. They said he had sung
the earth wide open and walked in,

either to bury her or to retrieve her,
and almost succeeded. They said when he slipped
he was on the way up; he ought to have known
not to look down.

Or they said he died like a midge,
of his own luminescence,
or it was darkness and light that he named
and they came together and killed him.

Still in the hills they tell simpler stories.
They say his voice shone
like a blue stone. Some of them say
it was air he drank when thirsty,

water he breathed. It may have been only
his hands, some of them say,
that gave way, crushed
when the words closed over them;

and for days his voice
could be seen overhead, next to the sun,
his words tasted in the wellwater,
wind out of season heard in the young grain.

All light since
has bent through his silence.

Since then it has been
the custom with musical
children
to put out the eyes.

CAVE OF THE NYMPHS

Daily, daily walking out of our eyes
in order to meet them returning,

the face full of acorns and mice,
the teeth pumping like heddles.

Daily peeping from under our tongues,
the ears like oars rowing backward and burning.

THE SALUTE BY TASTING

White water on the mountain,
cwms and seracs of the sea,
and the voice moving out like a small boat or a solitary climber,
too far away to see if it resembles
someone else or itself or yourself or me.

Between the bone and the unleashed blood:
the uncarved stone
and the landforms hammering gods
out of the godshapes of the air.
Between the hair that is the nail of the head
and the chin that is its heel:
brainleather, gunflint chert
and a broken ploughshare
heaped into a closed cup and triggered,
a cranium full of saltpeter and teeth, the mallet and anvil
detonator interwired with the ocular fuse.

Flutes, flutes,
flutes charming the chain
to rise like a serpent under the ball,
or the serpent's teeth to rise
like a wavering pillar under us all.

Between lover and lover, brother and brother,
other and other of you:
ropehold in the ravelling fissure.
Women and the broken gods
jut through the jumbled weather,
snagging the fibres of the jewel.
In the loose light's

118

glycerine-flow, metamorphic, between them, the rule.
Between one and one, one and other,
one neither one and one one another,
the use of love: to make the hate run true.

TWO VARIATIONS

I. ABSENCE OF THE HEART

Douceur d'être et de n'être pas — Valéry

Her footfalls, born of his voicelessness,
paving their way, like a saint's steps, patiently
lead, windchilled and mute,
toward the watchman's bed.

Shoeless like the gods, and the long light
laid across her arms.
All the words, all the silences disguised as words,
adrift between us and the unsaid.

Finally her lips close in, the invisible
nutrition of the kiss
opening the dark bouquet of mouths
fitted into his head.

Take your time. He has always been there
waiting, and his heart out stalking, still
when you are still and moving as you move,
matching your stride, echoing your tread.

II. THIN MAN WASHING

...et la terre mauvaise dans le champ de son coeur −Char

Once upon a time there was a man
who never hungered any more,
or so I heard – he had devoured so many legacies,
bitten off anything, eaten through anyone who came near –

who one day found
that his table was cleared,
his bed emptied, his children renamed,
and the soil gone sour in the uplands of his heart.

He had dug no grave; he had thought to survive.
He had nothing to give; he had less to receive.
Objects avoided him, animals lied to him,
the Diamond Sutra hung, untranslatable, on his wall.

It was only then that he crept back in
and stole hunger and shaped it into
a bowl, in which, to this day, when no one
is looking, and the wind not blowing, he bathes.

SIX EPITAPHS

Malmesbury, 881 A.D.,
Erigena, aged about seventy,
stabbed with a pen
in finibus mundi, for heresy.

*

Ephesos, 475 B.C.,
Herakleitos, called atrabilious, called
the obscure, sweating out his last fever
on the barnfloor, buried to the ears in warm manure.

*

Hunan, 289 B.C.,
Ch'ü Yüan, finding air insufficient
for certain syllables, taking
the springwater into his lungs.

*

Shensi, 90 B.C.,
Ssu-ma Ch'ien, his left hand hovering
where his balls had been
and his beard going, still pushing
the brush, bringing the record to its end.

*

Weimar, 1832 A.D., not
stared down, staring back, nor even
staring, gutbürgerlich Goethe simply
peering in at it, muttering
for more light, more light, more light, another angle.

*

Sicily, 456 B.C.,
a stone in the wheat stubble speaking
for Aeschylus, charging in summary: only
seacoast trees and surviving
enemies be permitted to praise him.

POEM WITHOUT VOICES

The light that blooms in your body
blooms in my hands. Around us the ground
is strewn with its petals.

I have seen on a street in Guadalajara
wind set the petals of a jacaranda
down on the ground surrounding a pine.

Love, this is evergreen. Let it be.
You will see, they fall also. Listen
again: the silences

ripen
deep in the sullen beaks
of the intricate wooden flowers.

BONE FLUTE BREATHING

Love, they say that a woman with steel-gray
eyes has lived for a thousand years
in these mountains. They say that the music
you almost hear in the level blue light
of morning and evening is music she played
in these mountains many years ago
on a flute she'd cut from the cannon bone
of a mule deer buck she'd tracked and wrestled
to the ground.
              They say that at the first few notes
she played, her sisters started giggling, because,
instead of listening, they were watching
the change that came over her face.
She stalked off in anger, and for years thereafter
only in darkness did anyone ever
hear the flute. Day after day
it lay silent on the mountain,
half hidden under a whitebark pine.
No one else was permitted to touch it,
much less to watch her while she played.

But a man came by one day from another
country, they say, who had never heard either
the flute or the story, and he found the flute
on the ground, under the pine tree, where it lay.
As soon as he put it to his lips, it played.
It breathed her music when he breathed,
and his hands began to find new
tunes between the tunes it played.

Angry once again at this intrusion,
the woman who lives in these mountains
complained about the stranger to her brother,
who lived on the other side of the world.

That very afternoon, her brother built
an elk's skull and antlers and a mountain cat's
intestines into a guitar, and as
he walked here, he taught himself to play.

Coming over the hills that way,
without a name, one stranger to another,
he challenged the stranger with the flute to a musical
duel to be judged by the woman who lives
in these mountains.
                    It may be the stranger, as many people
say, was simply unwary. It may be
the sun slivered his eyes that day
in such a way that he could see only
one choice. In any case, everyone
says that he consented to the contest.

They played night and day, and the stranger,
while he listened, watched the eyes,
and when they wandered, watched the lips
of the woman who lives in these mountains.
Sister, said the eyes. *Sister of the other
who is playing the guitar.* But the lips said, *Music
of the breath and music of the bone.* And the breath
of the woman, whether she willed it to or no,
kept moving in the flute whenever the stranger
played. After seven nights and days,
everyone knew the stranger was the winner.

That was when the man with the guitar said,
*Stranger, can you sing? Stranger, can you sing us
a song along with the music you play?
Listen,* said the man with the guitar,
and I will show you what I mean.
Then while the woman and the stranger watched
and listened, the man with the guitar stared
hard into the air, and his hands like water-spiders

126

flickered over the guitar, and a song slid
out between his teeth and flowed
through the music he played.

The stranger in his turn stared
hard into the air and far into the eyes
of the woman who lives in these mountains.
And the eyes stared back, and the eyes said, *Sister.*
Sister of the other who is playing the guitar.
Note after note he played, but no word
came. He stared long at her lips,
and the lips said, *Bone.* The lips said,
Wordless breath in the bone. And breathe
as he would, he could not
sing through the music he played.

So it was that the woman with the steel-gray
eyes, gazing into the whitebark
pine behind both of them, quietly declared
the man with the guitar to be the winner.

She reached for the flute,
but her brother stepped in front of her.
He picked up the flute and the guitar
and smacked them one against the other and against
the rocks until both of them shattered.

Then, taking the stranger by the throat,
he spun him flat against the ground,
and taking a splinter from the flute,
and moving swiftly, like a crouching
dancer, he peeled the living flesh
away from the stranger's feet and hands.
He peeled his face and hips and ribs
and carefully filleted each of his limbs.

One by one he extracted the stranger's
bones, and one by one he replaced them

with the splinters of the deerbone flute
and the shattered skull and antlers
which had been his own guitar.

He stitched the splinters into the stranger's
fingers, into his head and chest
and limbs with the mountain cat's intestines,
and set him on his feet, and propped the last splinter
of the bone flute upright in his hand,
and walked off, stopping to scrub
his own hands in a shrinking bank
of spring snow, never uttering a sound.

Love, the stranger stood there motionless
for years – but they say that the music you almost
hear in the level blue light of morning
and evening, now, is the sound of the stranger
moving, walking back toward his own country,
painfully, one step at a time.

Tzuhalem's Mountain

a sonata in three movements

I have set these poems of love and not-love under the name of a deformed man, out of a nagging feeling that they belong there. The spectre, and in due course the speaker, or one of the speakers, is a hunchbacked, sausage-mottled, dead Coast Salish Indian named Tzuhalem. Once I sailed into his cove – now on the charts as Genoa Bay – and camped looking up at his rock, still called Tzuhalem's Mountain.

Around 1830, leaders of the Halkomelem Salish villages near the mouth of the Cowichan River, on Vancouver Island, excommunicated and banished one of their own people. This exile was Tzuhalem, whom his elders had convicted in absentia of bride-theft and murder. The sentence must have been for judicial rather than practical effect, for Tzuhalem, if we may believe the tradition, had scarcely been seen in his native village for twenty years. He and his family, then estimated at fourteen wives and an unknown number of children, lived alone in the steep granite bluffs of what since then has been his mountain.

Some say that Tzuhalem acquired and kept his cluster of loves through occult means, others that he used more brutal physical methods. Whatever the case, in spite of his deformity there were women in his camp, and new ones among them every year. Though the sentence of banishment made him fair game, he was killed only in December 1854, at the age of about sixty – his head halved with a Hudson's Bay axe as he tried to kidnap yet another wife from one of the Gulf Islands.

I have nothing to add to his story. I have taken his name; and I have transported even that into other and higher mountains, elsewhere in the Salish country.

(And what of the sound and taste of that name? If we take the names of the dead in our mouths, shouldn't we do so in voices the dead might understand? The pronunciation of this one poses a problem for those who do not speak a Salish or Wakashan language, and who have not had phonetic training. The usual anglicization rhymes with *New Salem*.)

I. PARABLE OF THE THREE ROCKS

Love, I have seen in the mountains a man pluck
birdsnest lichen from the limb of an alpine
fir, where it hung in the wind like sea-green
goat hair; I have seen him gather three
white stones, as sharp and clear as milk teeth.

I have seen him lay these cracked
pieces of rock into the deep
cup of the nest like a creature
half hunter, half long-legged bird,

and seen him carry them away: three
razor-sharp stones: two
to stand for two lovers
and a third to stand for the world.

I have seen three razor-edged, milk-white
stones in a nest of sea-green lichen
on a table and heard them explained to inquisitive
visitors as the teeth of deep-water fishes
or the eggs of carnivorous birds.

II. PARABLE OF THE HARPS

Love, in the drum of the heart
are the hoofbeats of horses – the horse
of the muscles, the horse of the bones.

In the flutes of the bones are the voices
of fishes – the fish of the belly,
the fish of the fingers and limbs.

Love, in the stream of the limbs
we are swimming with fishes
and fording with lathering horses.

My love, in this bed full of horses
and fishes, I bring to the resonant gourds
of your breasts the harps of my hands.

III. PARABLE OF THE YEW TREES

Love, in this bed full of horses
and fishes, carnivorous birds
are leading us down into oceans
and up into mountains. My love,
in this bed full of horses and fishes,
carnivorous birds are screaming
their names and repeating their stories,
though no one can hear them.

They say we are falling like foraging
ospreys, they say we are climbing
like laddering salmon up out of the sea,
we are climbing like horses
up into the mountains filled with the sounds
of carnivorous birds. They say
we are carnivorous birds, climbing
up out of the mountains, climbing the air.

They say when we reach there
in the salt mirrors of your eyes
I will see only birds, and you
on the walls of my eyes only fishes.
They say in this bed full of fishes
and birds, all the men you have known
will ride through your face and fall
from their horses, drowning in sunlight and ashes,

the ospreys will dive and the salmon will climb
from the sea and the yew trees will lend us their voices,
though nothing we say with them then
will reach through those distances.

IV. BODY, SPEECH AND MIND

In the high passes the stones turn,
tuning the air. They are silent
who live there. As the cat
kills at the throat and then opens
the belly, those who can speak
lurk back toward the valley,
into the alder over the river,
where the air is played.

This is tuning and playing, love,
this is both, this is knowing and saying,
this is the dark heart of the bone
breathing like pine trees, this
is the heart like a claw in the ground.

This is the sound of the body
singing, the voice in its place,
under cliffs, by the bloodstream,
holding the skull in its outstretched
arms like an overturned bowl,
and singing, and singing
the song they dream near the rocks
in the difficult air.

V. PARABLE OF THE STREAM

Love, he has seen them
before, he has known
they were there,
scattered and gleaming.
Now in the clear
stream of your flesh
he is panning for bones.

VI. PARABLE OF THE THINKER

Love, in the bright
mirrors of your eyes
in the dark I have seen him
again: I have seen there
the great, angular
bird who feeds on your joy
as he feeds in the mountains
on the thinker's pain.

VII. PARABLE OF THE TWO BIRDS

I have seen in the mountains a shape
like two birds with three wings
between them, and seen them
swooping, seizing the same fish

from the stream and hovering
there until the shared wing
opened. I have seen the dark bone glide
like a knifeblade out of the feathers.

In the shadow of their wings I have seen then
the same thing happen to the fish:
the one bird suddenly clutching fins and flesh,
the other with the head and skeleton.

Love, the bird with the feathers took the flesh
of the fish and floated toward the ocean.
The bird with the bone wing rose
toward the peaks, and in his talons hung the skeleton.

Love, I have felt the world part in our hands.

§

VIII. FIRST LIGHT

Hawk and owl in the dead
red alder: daybird and nightbird asleep in the tree
while the spilt light builds in the snowchutes
high on the mountain.

Unopened, like roses,
the milk-smooth, identical faces
of those I have loved for the eloquence
of their pain.

IX. QUESTIONS FOR THE OLD WOMAN

From the hills of your breasts to the ruined wells
of your eyes is how many miles, old woman?
And how many days to the outwash fans
and gravelled channels of your thighs?

Old woman, what do we know but the swollen
thumb of the tongue against the cranium?
What do we know but the bloodshot
knuckles of the eyes,

the sting of the light in the tightening
fist, the ache of the darkness caked
in the hand? What do we know but the innocent
songs of the lungs in their cage never mating?

What do we know but the dry rasp
of a banjo pick against paper, the whisper
of blood against wood in the stunted trunk
of a tree, uprooted and running?

X. STALKING THE EARTHLUTE

Old woman, the hungry
ghosts as they gather
lick dry lips and gibber
against your thighs.
What will you
say as you chase them
away? You can neither
ignore them nor feed them.
Your fingers are chanting
already to chase them
away, and what
will you say? They are singing
with swollen tongues,
the dead are dying
of thirst, the dead
are dying of thirst,
with swollen tongues
in their broken lips
they are singing. They say
if I play you will sing me
a song of the flesh,
old woman, the wisdom
of fish who swim up
from the ocean, the wisdom
of birds who return
to their tundra
year after year
down the winding canyons
of the air, the immense
wisdom, old woman,
of trees who remain
in their places, embracing
the earth, the wisdom
in summer of hummingbirds,

mouth to mouth
in the air with the open-mouthed
flowers, the ripe
sisters surrounded
by rubbernecked brothers,
old woman, the wisdom
of men who emerge
from the sea and descend
through the mouths of the mountain.
Old woman, they say
you will sing if I play
on the unstrung lute
of your back, on the cracked
piano built
of your bones, on the wrinkled
guitar in the threadbare
case of your body.
Old woman, the banjo
hangs like an arrowless
bow in your belly,
but they say if I can play it
you will sing. They say
you will sing me
the words of the song.

XI. SONG OF TZUHALEM

Belly and back
beak of the bird
claw of the cat
plucking the taut

muscle and gut
beak of the bird
belly and back
claw of the cat

plucking the taut
muscle and gut
claw of the cat
belly and back

beak of the bird
plucking the taut
muscle and gut
belly and back

beak of the bird
claw of the cat
plucking the taut
muscle and gut

belly and back
beak of the bird
beak of the bird
claw of the cat

XII. HIC AMOR, HAEC PATRIA

Old woman, a man
comes into the mountains
alone in high summer
because he is eaten.
His body is eaten
by darkness in winter,
his mind is eaten
in spring by the deepening
pulse of his hunger.
The bees know his blood
on the hillside in summer
as bright as red heather.
The birds, old woman,
the birds, the birds,
the birds know his blood
on the mountain in autumn
as black as empetrum.

Old woman, a man
comes into the mountains
to make himself whole.
Why is it the knife
of love redivides us?
Why is it a man
cannot heal the wounds
in a woman by bringing
her also up into
these mountains?

Old woman, old woman,
her body like water,
her flesh like a fish,

the wind in the air
underlying her name.

All knowledge is carnal.
Knowledge is meat,
knowledge is muscle.
Old woman, old woman,
what is this hunger
grown hard as a bone?

XIII. LONICERA INVOLUCRATA

Mouth to mouth, our faces
closing one another's faces,
the lids of our skulls
closing one another's eyes.

And the ghosts of the butterscotch eyes
of Tzuhalem in pairs in the twilight
like twinberry flowers.
Ghosts of his women
probe for their nectar like needle-beaked birds.

The waxwing sits
in the willow tree, waiting.

In the wilted light,
the beaten blue metal of the sea.

XIV. LAST LIGHT

Herons croak from the broken hemlocks.
Herons glide beneath Tzuhalem's
mountain. The heart, like a bat going out
after moths in the shadows, unfolds and floats singing

to rocks, trees and its prey, its shrill
but inaudible syllables pulsing and quickening,
eats, and retreats once again to the stench
of its cave, strung up by one foot, with the other foot

bathing.

§

XV. PARABLE OF THE MOON

In the cave of the moon
thirteen women are moving.
At new moon a man
with three shoulders will rise
and move with them, his three-shouldered
dancing joined to their dancing
in front of the fire.

XVI. PARABLE OF THE TRUTH

Love, I love, I
do not love, no,
it is true, I do not
love, but I love you
anyway, as well
as I am able
in these difficult
conditions. What
can a man come back
to say, who does not
know the word
hello, who never said
goodbye, and also
does not know
if he has ever reached
or left his destination?

XVII. PARABLE OF THE VOICES

Behind the heart
is a deaf musician
beating a broken
drum. He is watching
the animals leap
through the hoops of our voices.

The air is another
earth full of burrows
the animals enter
and leave through the doors
of our voices. Down through our voices
the waterbirds dive.

XVIII. HIS DREAM

In his hands is a face
full of fossils and pebbles.
A mask. It comes out of
the lake where a man
who is dying is trying
to drown and keeps failing.

The faces afloat
on the water are never
his own. When they shatter
he holds them together.

They show him the mask.
He goes with them, and when
he returns, all the faces
he sees are like faces
in water. They shatter.
He holds them together.

He calls to his sister
to help him. She baits
a fishline with feathers
and casts, and the faces

come up from the water
and shatter. Out of
the jagged pieces
of faces, she gathers
the mask. When he wears it,
his hands twitch like rattles.

XIX. PARABLE OF THE LAKE'S EDGE

Old woman, a man
must stand on his shadow
to fish from the shore
of the lake of the daylight.
Morning and evening
his shadow is moving.
Morning after morning
a man must rename
the sun without breathing.
Morning after morning
a man standing still
as a stick at the lake's edge
must gather the dance
in his hands without moving.

XX. PARABLE OF THE INDESTRUCTIBLE

Where is it now, the golden bough
I carried through her body?
Where is the taste of sweet water
torn from our mouths? And why is it

the birds who can sing never enter
the water or hunt from the mountain?
Listen: the bleat of the widgeon,
the moan of the loon and the croak of the heron,

the hawks howling like wolves and the sea eagles
neighing like horses, the gibber of gulls,
and the small owl barking in daylight:
like bones in their throats their own

indestructible questions.

XXI. PARABLE OF THE SUN

Bright fish in the shallows
breaking their guts to come home to these gravels,
their bowels chewed by the unborn,
their backs by the eagles.

The man in the sun, savaged
by cats, drags his cloak through the waters
and limps up the mountain,
his footprints in tatters.

GLOSSARY

BIRDSNEST LICHEN   *Alectoria sarmentosa*, also called, in spite of its pale green color, Old Man's Beard. It is ubiquitous in the subalpine forests of the Coast Range, where it grows, along with the darker lichen called Bear's Hair (*Bryoria* spp.), in the branches of conifers.

CADURCIAN   The black wine of Cahors, like everything else from that city, is known as Cadurcian, just as people and things from Aix-en-Provence are called Aquisextain and those from Glasgow Glaswegian.

CHINQUAPIN   *Castanopsis chrysophylla*, a tree of the Siskiyou and Trinity Mountains. Petrarca, alas, can never have seen one, though he must have known its close relative the European chestnut, *Castanea sativa*, whose similar spined pod is nearly as dangerous to the hands of men and the feet of horses.

CWM   A glaciated alpine valley or cirque.

EARTHLUTE   One of the simplest of musical instruments: strings stretched over the mouth of a hole in the ground, so that the whole earth serves as the resonator.

EL-ARISH   A town on the north coast of the Sinai, not far from Gaza. Until the Six Day War, it was the site of one of several anti-aircraft emplacements in the peninsula, where Egyptian radar, gun and missile crews were in training under Soviet advisors. Weeks and months after that quickest and least conclusive of wars, the soldier-students' manuscript notes, on everything from elementary calculus to techniques of chemical warfare, lay in the sand with the bodies and boots and spare parts like finds of papyri. The machine-gun in the poem is the Israeli Uzi, and the radar a Russian mobile, known as Fan-Song to NATO.

EMPETRUM *Empetrum nigrum*, an evergreen alpine plant—known also as crowberry or crakeberry, for the dry black fruits which follow its somber flowers.

EURYTOS A Presocratic mentioned by Theophrastos and Aristotle. He tried, it seems, more literally than anyone before or since, to picture the world in numerical terms.

HIC AMOR, HAEC PATRIA "Love here, land there." With these words among others, Aeneas takes leave of Dido, whom he has jilted.

HIPPOLYTUS (*c*. 170–235) A bishop at Rome, later exiled to Sardinia. His book, *Philosophoumena*, traces a number of Christian heresies to Presocratic roots, and in so doing unwittingly preserves otherwise unavailable fragments of the early Greek thinkers.

IN FINIBUS MUNDI "At the edge of the world": a medieval prelate's description of the British Isles.

ITZEHECAIAN, TLALOCAN, ILHUICAC "Obsidian Wind, Tlalocland, Daylight." These are the Nahuatl names of the three regions of the afterlife in the Aztec cosmology.

LEDA The Greek storytellers said that a woman of this name was raped by Zeus, who assumed the form of a swan for this purpose. Later in the day her husband, Tyndareos, King of Lakonia, also took her to bed, and this accounts for the fact that her daughters—Helen of Troy, who was kidnapped by Paris, and Klytaimnestra, who married and later murdered Agamemnon—were hardly identical, though they were twins. One, the very beautiful Helen, had been sired by Zeus, and the other twin by Tyndareos.

LEMURIBUS VERTEBRATIS, OSSIBUS INTER TENEBRAS "For the vertebrate ghosts, for the bones among the darknesses."

LONICERA INVOLUCRATA   The coast twinberry, a bush of the honeysuckle family. Its binocular yellow flowers are followed by bright black fruits staring in pairs from blood-colored collars. The berries, though bitter to the human palate, are a favorite food of cedar waxwings.

MILETOS   A city in Ionian Greece, the home of Thales and his famous pupils, Anaximander and Anaximenes, who together formed the "Milesian school" of Greek thought.

$1 + e^{\pi i} = 0$ "One plus e to the power pi-i equals zero": an identity established by Roger Cotes shortly before his death in 1716, and again independently by Leonhard Euler about 1740. The components are two transcendental irrationals, e and π, together with a "lateral" (in Gauss's phrase) or "imaginary" (according to Descartes) number represented by the letter i. More specifically, π is the circumference of a circle of unit diameter, $= 3.14159\ldots$; e is the base of the so-called natural or hyperbolic logarithms, $= 2.71828\ldots$; and $i = \sqrt{-1}$, a number so vexing to Leibnitz that he labelled it "an amphibian between being and non-being."

PHEREKYDES   A contemporary of Thales and Herakleitos, living at Syros in the Cyclades: one more of the many Greek philosopher-poet-physicists of his age.

PHOKAIA   A city in Ionian Greece. Elea, on the Tyrrhene coast of southern Italy, where Parmenides was born, was then a new Phokaian colony.

PTAHHOTEP   (c. 2400 B.C.) A government minister under Isesi at Memphis, 5th Dynasty. A collection of maxims under his name survives in several versions, notably in Papyrus Prisse (Bibliothèque nationale). Three or four lines of that text appear in the poem as a kind of refrain.

SSU-MA CH'IEN   Historian, author of the *Shih Chi*. After speaking too boldly in front of the emperor, he was sentenced to castration – an invitation, in the custom of the time, to take his own life instead. But Ssu had not yet finished his book. To the court's consternation, therefore, he accepted the punishment and went on with his writing.

TEZCATLIPOCA   See next entry.

TLALOC   "Four Glyphs" is a brief meditation on four of the Aztec gods: 1) Tlaloc, "He in the Land," whose nearest counterpart in the Indo-European tradition is probably Poseidon; 2) Quetzalcoatl, the Feathered Lizard or, in D.H. Lawrence's more famous phrase, the Plumed Serpent, who inhabits the mask of Ehecatl, the wind, and is the drunken savior; 3) Huitzilopochtli, "Hummingbird from the Left," who drinks blood for the sun; and 4) Tezcatlipoca, the Smoking Mirror, the impalpable transformer, who in some accounts is not one god but four brothers. These four in their turn are Xipe Totec the Red, Lord of the Flayed Skin; Tezcatlipoca himself, the wizard, whose color is black; and two others we have already met: Quetzalcoatl the White and Huitzilopochtli the Blue.

TSO CHUAN   The commentary of Tso-ch'iu Ming on the *Ch'un Ch'iu* or *Spring and Autumn Annals*, third century B.C.

URBAN   Guillaume de Grimoard, who reigned as Pope Urban V from 1362 until his death in 1370. In 1367 he returned the papacy to Rome from Avignon. Petrarch thinks of following him via the old Roman road through Firenze, the Via Cassia.

VARÈSE, EDGARD   (1883 – 1965) French-born composer who immigrated to the USA in 1915. One of his finer and more famous compositions is *Density 21.5*, for solo flute. Another is the "electronic poem" entitled *L'Homme et la machine*.

ACKNOWLEDGEMENTS

This selection is drawn in part from the following books and chapbooks: *The Shipwright's Log* (Kanchenjunga Press, 1972); *Cadastre* (Kanchenjunga, 1973); *Deuteronomy* (Sono Nis Press, 1974); *Eight Objects* (Kanchenjunga, 1975); *Bergschrund* (Sono Nis, 1975); *Jacob Singing* (Kanchenjunga, 1977); *The Stonecutter's Horses* (Standard Editions: William Hoffer & the Pulp Press, 1979); and *Tzuhalem's Mountain* (Oolichan Books, 1982). Poems collected here for the first time have been published as broadsides by Slug Press ("The Salute by Tasting") and the University of British Columbia Library ("Death by Water"), and in several periodicals and anthologies: *Arion*; *Canadian Literature*; *Handbook*; *Kayak*; *The Malahat Review*; *Pearl*; *Prism International*; *Queen's Quarterly*; *Saturday Night*; *Aurora* (Doubleday, 1978); *The Pushcart Prize IV* (Pushcart Press, 1979); and *News and Weather* (Brick Books, 1982).